OBEY

STAY ASLEEP

CONSUME

BUY

DO NOT QUESTION AUTHORITY

WATCH T. V.

NO IMAGINATION

MARRY AND REPRODUCE

NO
INDEPENDENT
THOUGHT

SUBMIT

CONFORM

REWARD
INDIFFERENCE

NO FUTURE

MONEY IS YOUR GOD

YOU ARE
NOTHING

DO NOT PROTEST

HONOR APATHY

WORSHIP CELEBRITIES

WORK 8 HOURS
SLEEP 8 HOURS
PLAY 8 HOURS

DOUBT
HUMANITY

YOU ARE A VICTIM

GREED IS GOOD

WAR IS PEACE

GENDER IS A CONSTRUCT

ART IS TERRORISM

FREEDOM IS ILLUSION

VOTE A OR B

DON'T THINK

FOLLOW THE LEADER

DRUG YOURSELF

PAY YOUR TAXES

HAVE SEX WITH EVERYTHING

TRUST NOBODY

RESISTANCE IS FUTILE

LIVE IN FEAR

EAT

BIG BROTHER IS WATCHING

WATCH PORN

WORK UNTIL RETIREMENT

THEN KILL YOURSELF

GIVE UP

www.ingramcontent.com/pod-product-compliance
Lightning Source LLC
Chambersburg PA
CBHW081538280526
45788CB00010B/3279